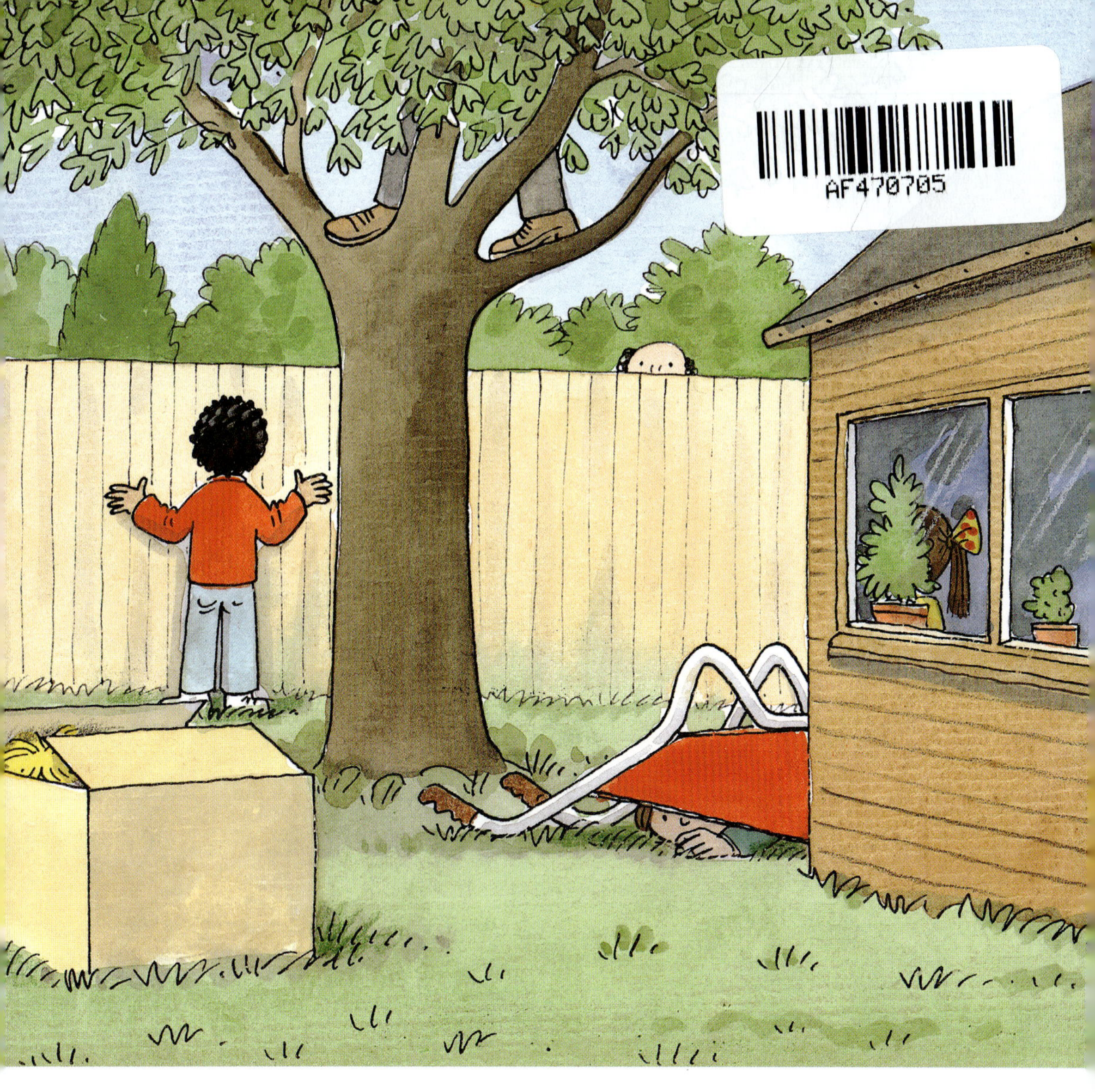

Can you see us?

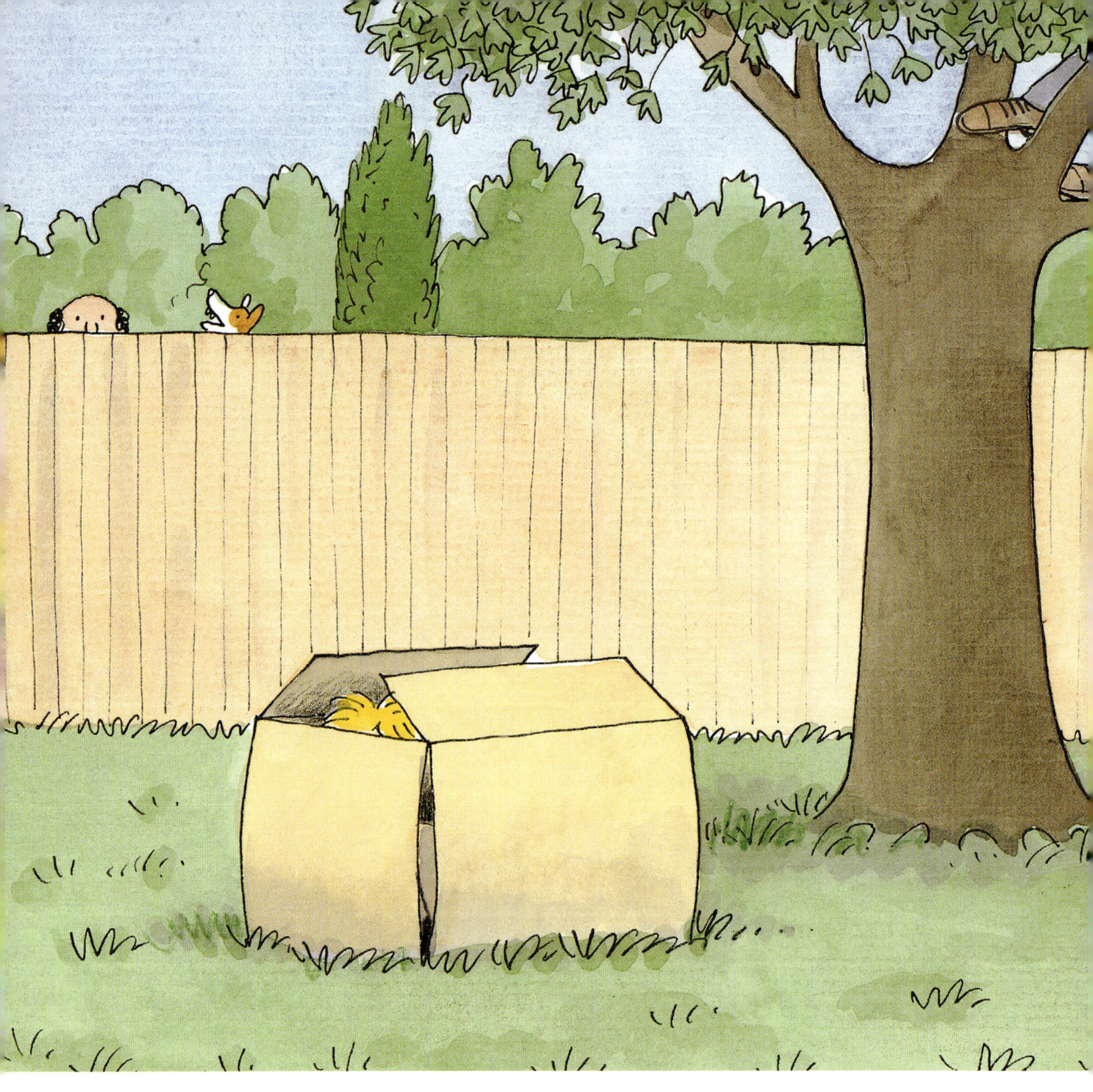

Can you see me?

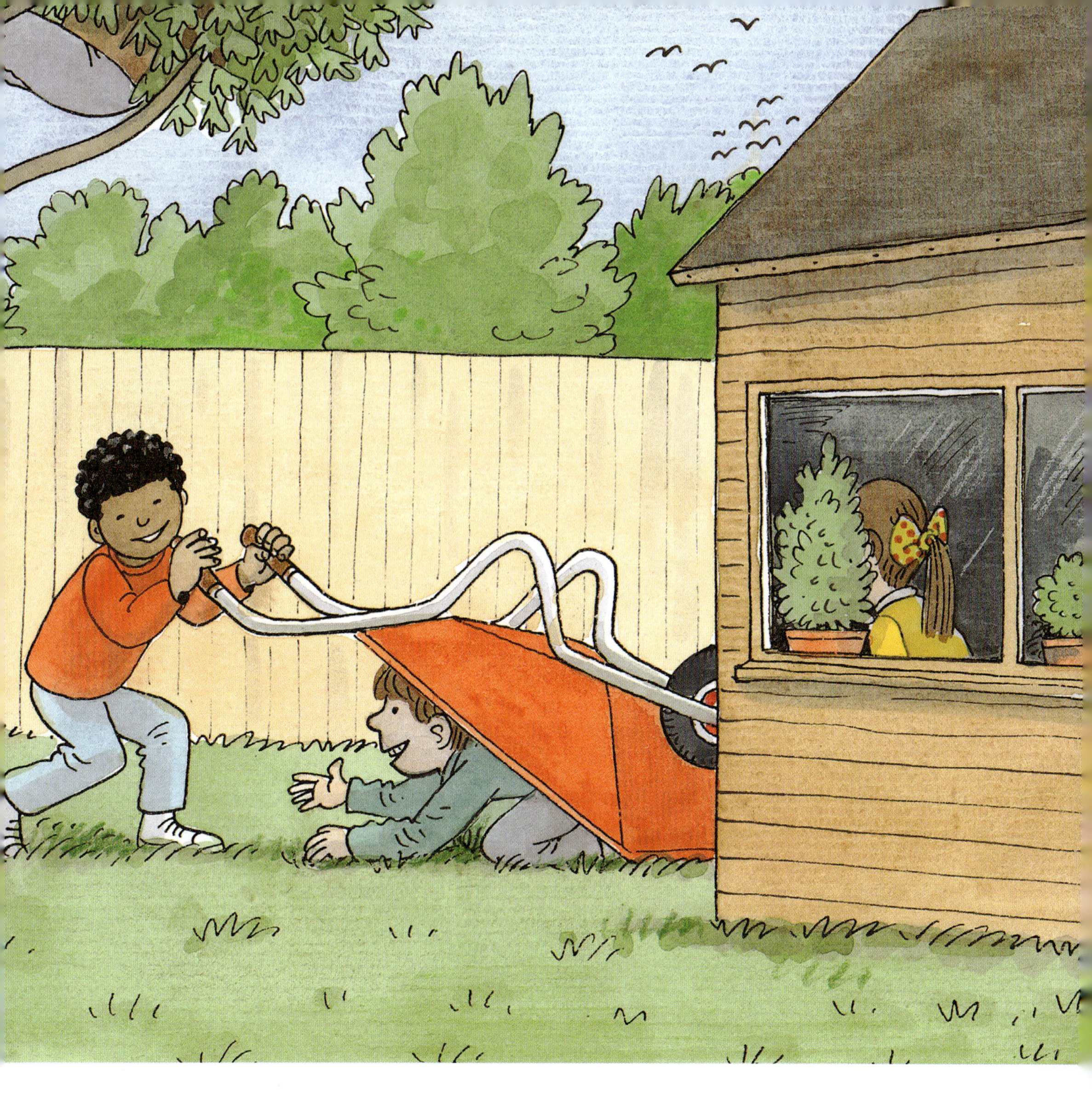

Yes, I can see you.

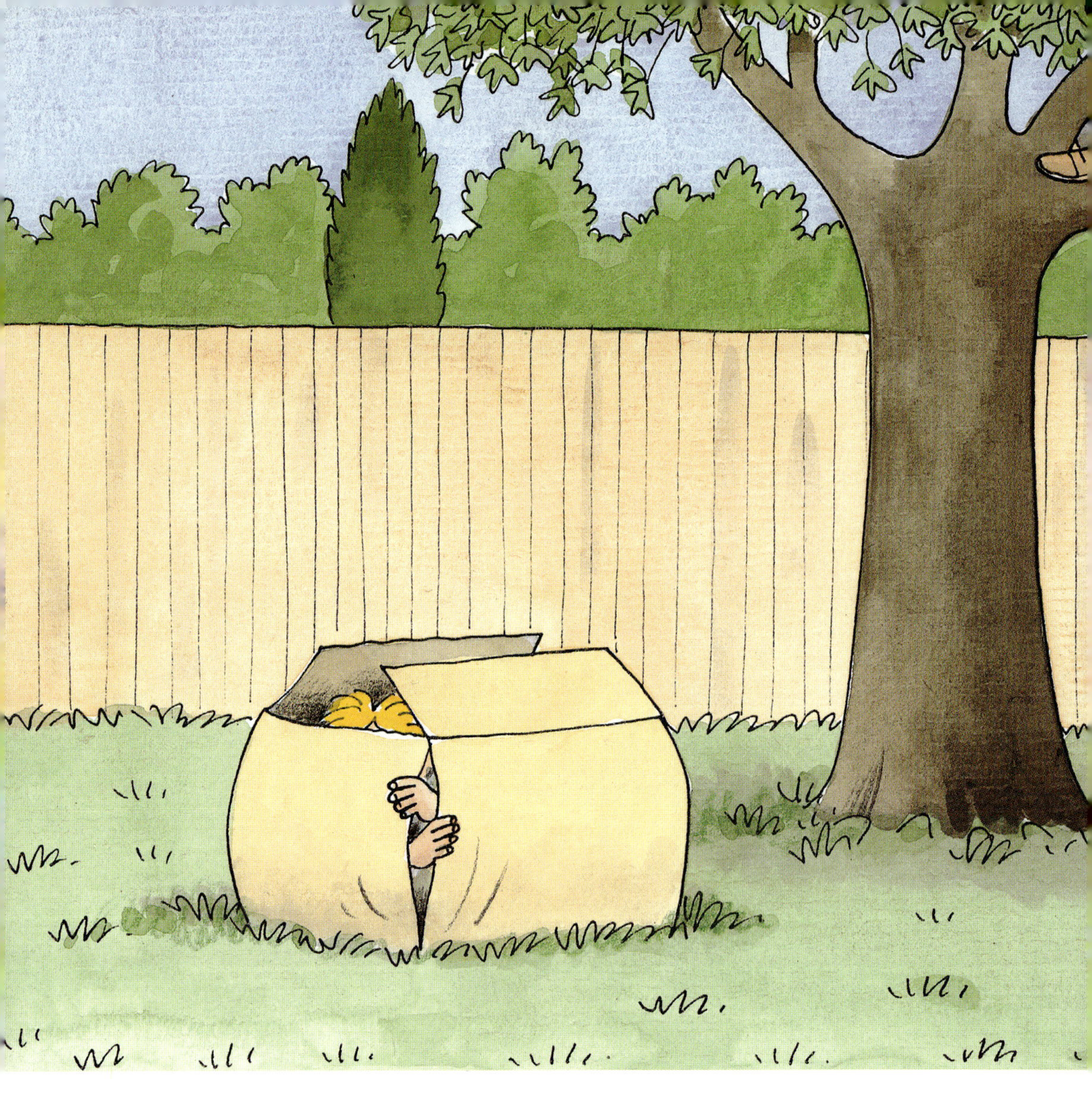

Can you see me?

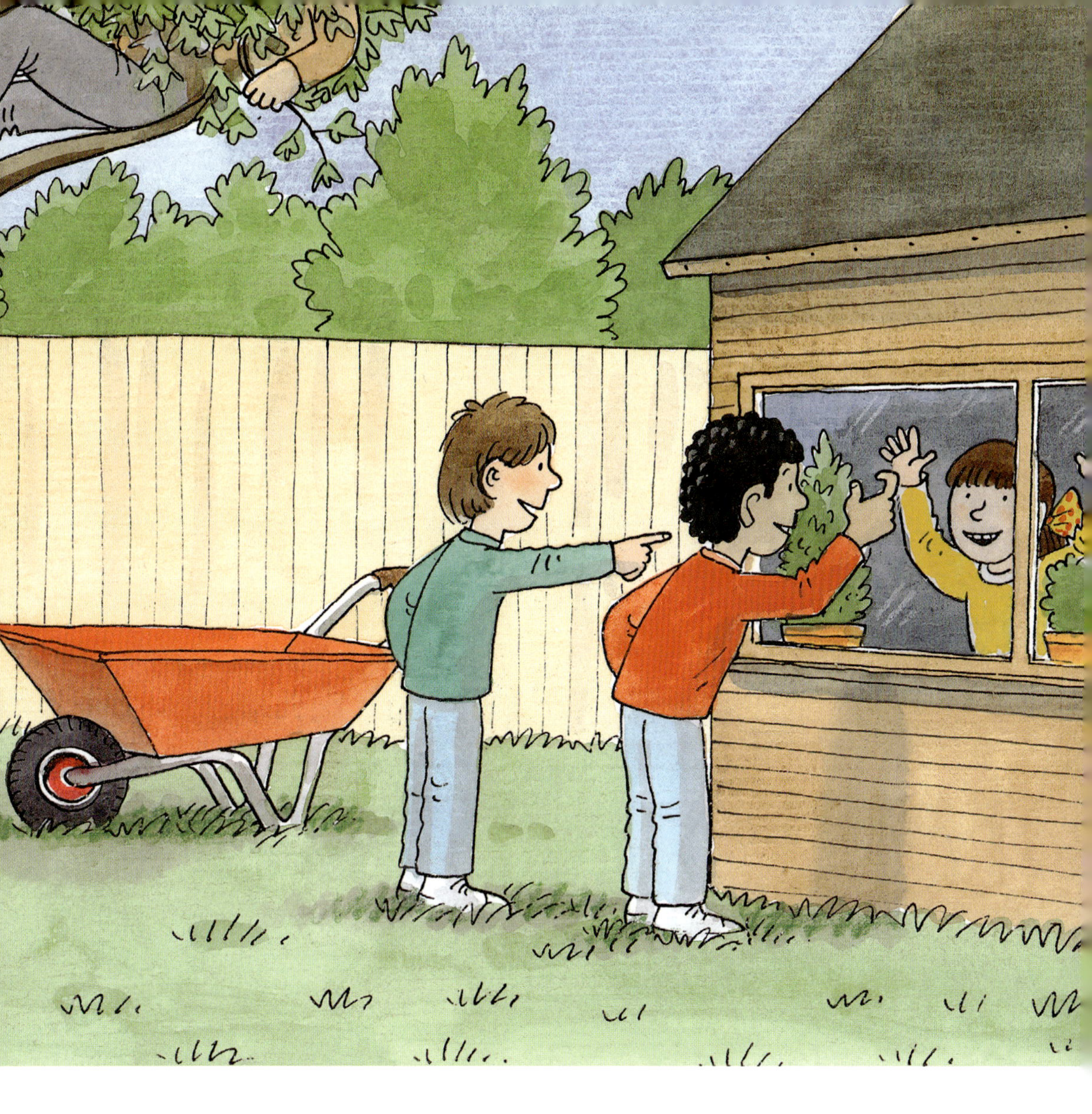

Yes, we can see you.

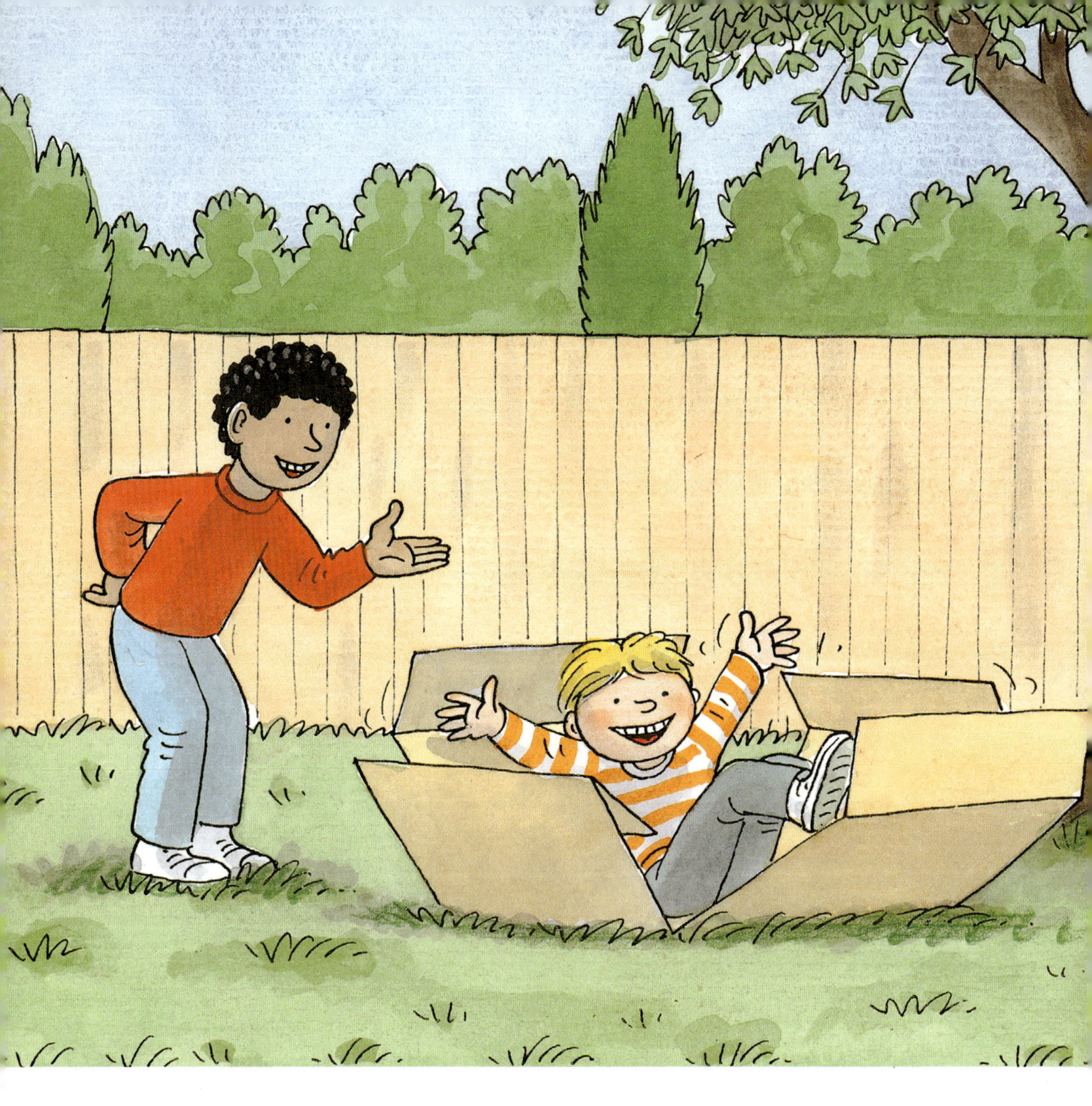

Can you see me?

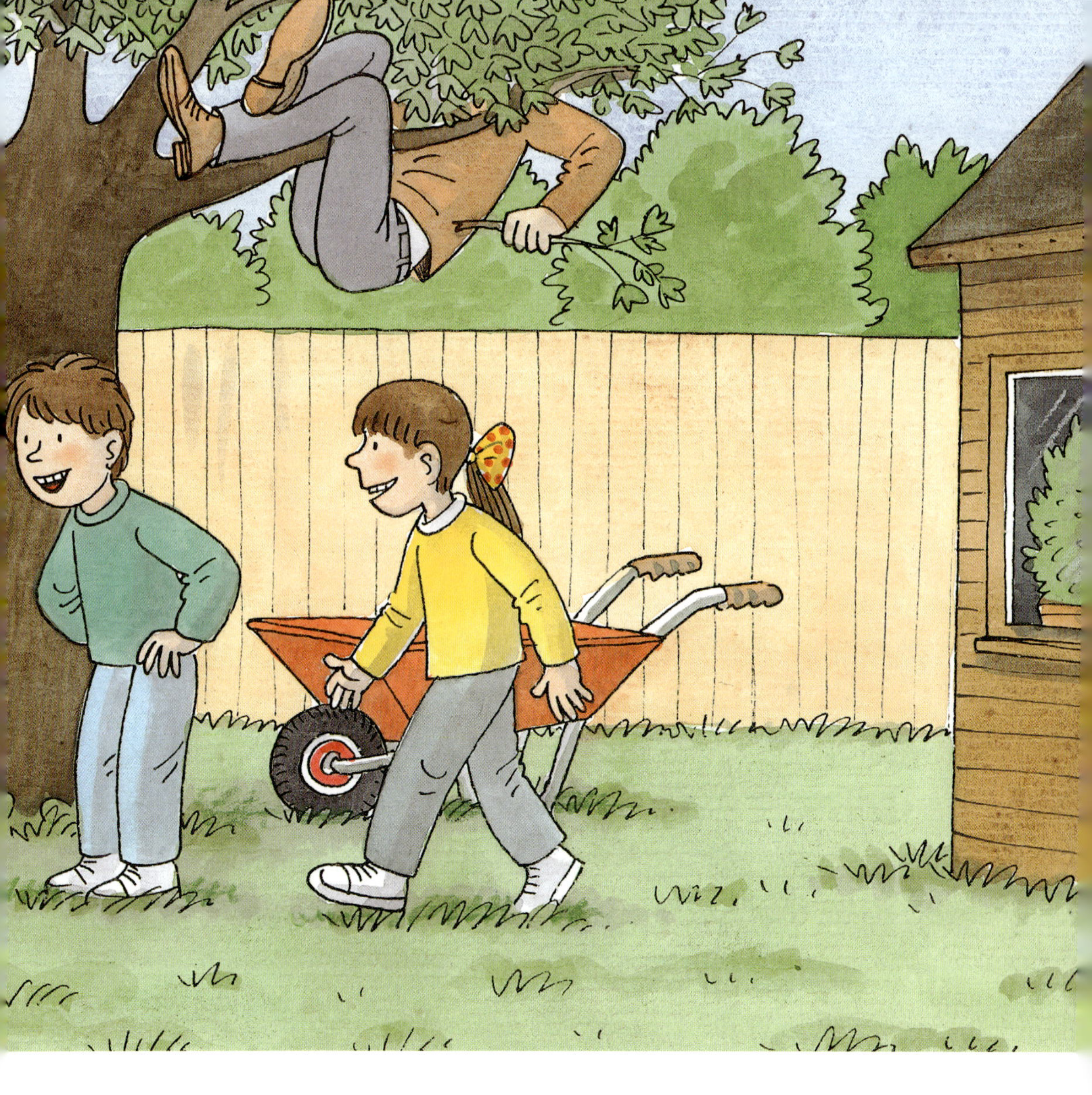

Yes, we can see you.

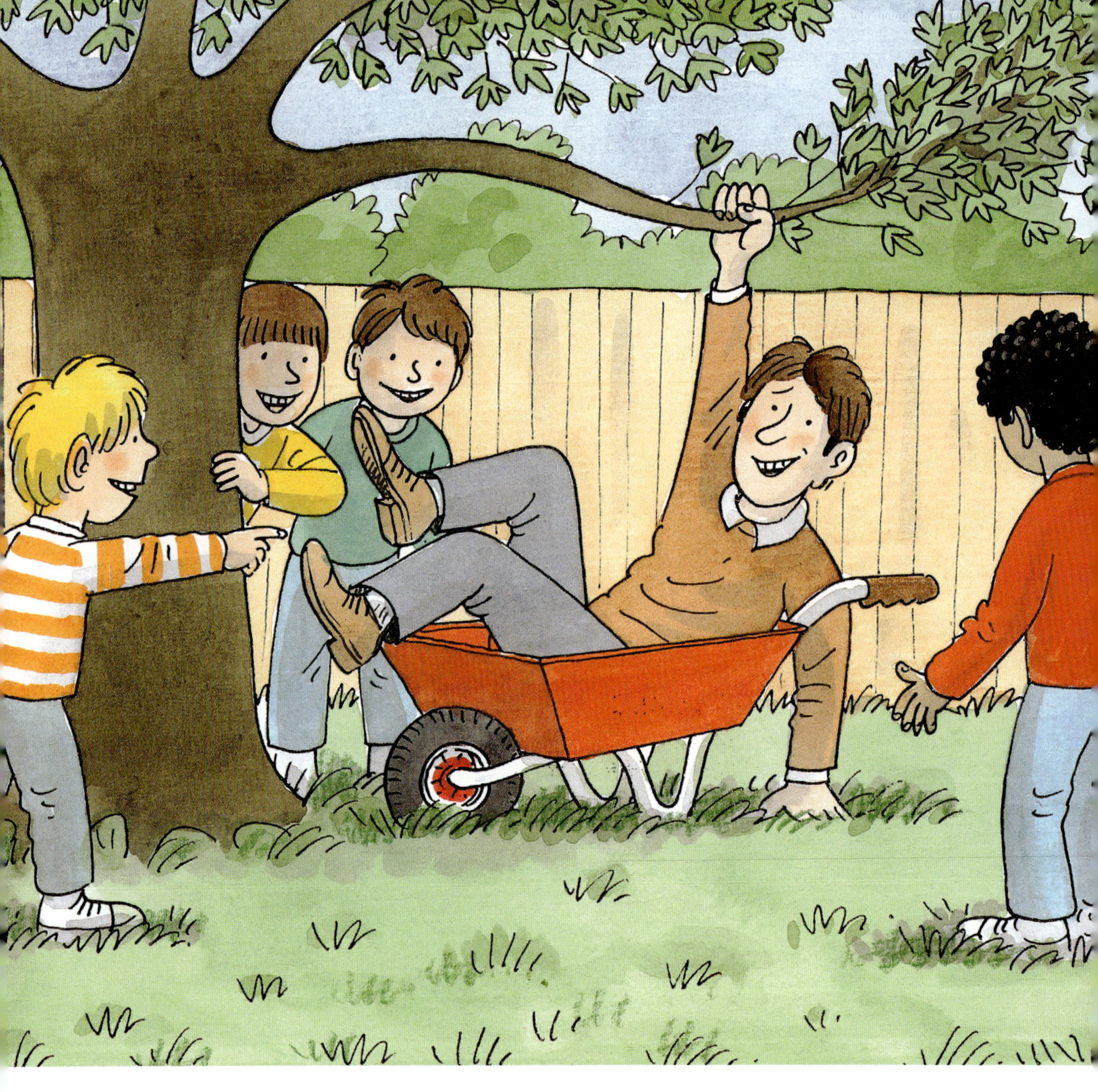

We can all see Dad.